an ordinary woman

marlene marburg

© Marlene Marburg 2005, 2017.

This book is copyright.
Reproduction of poems, prayers, artwork or any other content from this book is not permitted without the expressed permission of the author. Inquiries can be made to the publisher.

Published by Windsor Scroll Publishing
PO Box 6024 Doncaster 3108 AUSTRALIA
www.marlenemarburg.com.au

Second edition printed and bound by IngramSpark.

THE HOLY BIBLE, NEW INTERNATIONAL VERSION®, NIV® Copyright © 1973, 1978, 1984, 2011 by Biblica, Inc.™ Used by permission. All rights reserved worldwide.

Poems, text and artwork: Marlene Marburg
Cover design and layout: Cameron Semmens, www.webcameron.com

National Library of Australia Cataloguing-in-Publication entry:
An Ordinary Woman.
Marlene Marburg
ISBN 0 9586114 2 4 (original edition)
ISBN 978-0-9586114-7-3 (second edition)
1. Spirituality 2. Poetry

If we love each other enough, we will bear with each other's faults and burdens. If we love enough, we are going to light that fire in the hearts of others. And it is love that will burn out the sins and hatreds that sadden us.[1]
— DOROTHY DAY

Contents

Foreword	6
Companion Mary	9
How Can This Be?	11

Joy — **13**

Yes	14
In Grace …	18
In You God	19
Mary Visits Elizabeth	20
I Hope	22
The Birth of Jesus	23
According to Joseph	25
Sealed	26
Jesus Is Presented to God	27
Summoned	29
Mary and Joseph Find Jesus in the Temple	30
That Day	33

Light — **35**

Jesus Is Baptized	36
The Best Wine	39
The Good News	43
Living Water	45
Christ the Light	47
Who Is My Mother?	50
Unclenched	52
Body of Christ	54
We Come …	57
This Bread	58
Listen … I Am	60

Suffering — 61

- Decision in the Garden — 62
- Oh Judas — 64
- Are You a King? — 65
- Jesus Is Flogged — 66
- Jesus Is Crowned with Thorns — 68
- The Cross — 70
- Earthed — 73
- The Carpenter — 74
- God — 75
- Jesus Dies — 76
- Silent — 79
- In the Rain — 80

Revelation — 81

- Mary at Home — 82
- Risen — 83
- Mary's Prayer — 85
- She Who Saw — 86
- An Appearance to the Disciples — 87
- Jesus at God's Right Hand — 89
- Peace I Leave with You — 91
- The Presence of the Holy Spirit — 94
- Naming God — 96
- Prayer — 97
- God — 99
- With You Jesus — 100

About The Author — 102
Also by The Author — 103
References — 104

Foreword

Thank you to readers of *an ordinary woman* and those who requested this second edition. There are some differences to the first edition; for example, this edition uses the *New International Version* of the Bible. The layout, content and images are also changed. The spiritual orientation is contemporary and inclusive.

The idea of *an ordinary woman* emerged in 2004 from reflection and journaling during the thirty-three weeks of engaging with the Spiritual Exercises of Saint Ignatius of Loyola.[2] These exercises offer a way to deepen a person's awareness of the Mystery of God's presence and power in everyday life.

As I began the exercises, I desired a deepening awareness of the companionship of God as Source of life. I also sought deeper graced encounters with the Jesus of the Gospels. However the journey with Mary, the mother of Jesus, came as a gift I did not expect. Even today as I write this second edition, I am still surprised by the gift of Mary during those weeks.

In *an ordinary woman* imaginative contemplation built on gospel narratives, is foundational to Mary's conversations with God entitled "In Mary's Heart". Imagination, one of the intricate attributes which make us human, is a gift. Imagination cannot be contrived. Allowing prayer to emerge from the imagination is similar to the experience of dreaming wherein subconscious deep desires, hopes and fears are enacted and awareness is raised. This kind of prayer has the potential to enrich one's understanding of the way God wants to be in communion with the world, especially the world of relationships. It can inspire or motivate people towards creative action in the service of others.

I encourage you to engage your imagination as you meet God in prayer. If you are reluctant to contemplate imaginatively, you might like to read the texts and relax into God's Presence. I am ever amazed at the variety of ways which humans are drawn more deeply into the Mystery of Love.

Mary's relationship with God is pivotal in the book. She is portrayed as an ordinary and unique woman trying to love her son through the turns and twists of their lives. Women and men alike can relate with Mary through her breadth of feelings and thoughts as well as her moments of dedication and passion wherein she experiences the companionship of God or the silence, even absence, of God.

Throughout *an ordinary woman*, Mary speaks the name 'God' as a poetic attempt at naming Mystery. In Jewish tradition no-one speaks the name of God. This respectful practice reveres the truth that 'God' is unable to be contained in any human construct. YHWH, a biblical reference to God, which Christians sometimes change into Yahweh, is at best poetic. It has no vowels and is an unutterable combination of letters.

An ordinary woman is divided into four main sections which follow the life, death and renewal cycle characteristic of all of life. The book includes scripture, imaginative contemplation, prayerful conversations, quotes, poems, a few images and many suggestions for reflection. The poems contain traditional or contemporary content related to the texts.

Intended for individuals or groups, *an ordinary woman* is prayer material to be pondered over as many days as you choose. I hope the material will assist you to encounter Jesus, Mary his mother and other gospel characters with increasing personal relevance. It will surely help you to encounter the wonder of yourself.

As you read this book, you might write your own reflections on your prayer experience. Prayerful journal writing can enable personal growth and freedom.

So I present this second edition to you with delight and with the invitation to allow *an ordinary woman* to open to you the much greater invitation from the Mystery of life to live in abundant love. I hope that God will gift you with the joy of a personal journey you did not expect.

Companion Mary

> *There is a holiness about our life and its details. There is holiness in our birth and holiness in such mundane activities as sitting here before the computer monitor or bathing or eating breakfast or washing dishes. The divine is present when we are with our families and friends and doing our work and enjoying our recreation, and God will be with us still in that sacred moment when we take our last breath.*[3]

At times, theological statements have put holiness and ordinariness, or sacred and profane, as polar opposites. Some commentaries equate ordinariness with sinfulness. There are problems with all definitions which put any concepts or even actions as polar opposites. Is it not God's life constitutive to humanity that enables a spectrum of ideas, including sinful ideas, to be thought and enacted? If, as I suggest, sinfulness is an intentional abuse, albeit partial, of human creative capacities, or a disengagement at some level with the Mystery of life either through corrupt actions or as a posture for living, we can claim that ordinariness in human life is the holiness of living humanity fully. In this view, sin is a blot on ordinary personhood. It is an abuse of God's creative capacity in humanity.

Mary's yes to God is a yes to personhood. It is a yes to co-creation. Love came through her yes and the subsequent yeses she expressed and enacted in God throughout her life. In an ordinary woman, Mary is revealed as a person who is attentive to life and who wants to live in creative union with God. Mary is faithful to personhood through embracing the breadth and depth of experience which life's events and circumstances offer.

Mary models a discerning life. In the meditations, she acts in responsible love, showing us how to stand by our loved ones as they grow into their identities; as they move away from the family home trusting their capacity to pursue and fulfil dreams; as they make decisions which have repercussions of which grief is one.

Mary is an ordinary woman, empowered, graced and consoled in the presence of Mystery. Mary shows herself to be a good companion, a partner in prayer and an understanding friend.

How Can This Be?

You forget what was said.

You are in the present,
surrendering to another
incomprehensible image.

Synapses surge and ebb.
Your thoughts soaked at
                hightide
from the sea, your soul.

Your tongue accomplishes –
How can this be?

You speak to someone
a companion
Perhaps one of the selves.

You resist the rush
wave after wave.

You do not ask why
or put forward a deal if.
You ask for science.

You speak
one ordinary
yet astonishing word –
Yes.

Joy

Attention is the beginning of devotion.[4]
— Mary Oliver

Yes

In the sixth month of Elizabeth's pregnancy, God sent the angel Gabriel to Nazareth, a town in Galilee, to a virgin pledged to be married to a man named Joseph, a descendant of David. The virgin's name was Mary. The angel went to her and said, "Greetings, you who are highly favored! The Lord is with you." Mary was greatly troubled at his words and wondered what kind of greeting this might be. But the angel said to her, "Do not be afraid, Mary; you have found favor with God. You will conceive and give birth to a son, and you are to call him Jesus. He will be great and will be called the Son of the Most High. The Lord God will give him the throne of his father David, and he will reign over Jacob's descendants forever; his kingdom will never end." "How will this be," Mary asked the angel, "since I am a virgin?" The angel answered, "The Holy Spirit will come on you, and the power of the Most High will overshadow you. So the holy one to be born will be called the Son of God. Even Elizabeth your relative is going to have a child in her old age, and she who was said to be unable to conceive is in her sixth month. For no word from God will ever fail. "I am the Lord's servant," Mary answered. "May your word to me be fulfilled." Then the angel left her. (Lk1:26-38. See also Gen18:14).

Conversation with Mary

Mary, I am curious about the way life is unfolding for you. Why would you believe God is asking you, a child-woman, to be a mother? I wonder generally about parents and children; is this fate? Is this God's initiative?

So how was it for you, Mary? What happened when you recognized God's request in your heart? What did you feel? What did you know? And what happened in your questioning moments?

Many women keep the news of pregnancy to themselves for a while. There are also women who feel ashamed that they are not pregnant. There are women and men who remain single, living with a breadth of feelings about child-bearing, having children and parenting. What was it like for you, Mary? How did you feel? Were you frightened? Were you ashamed? Was there a part of you wanting to shout the news: *I am going to become a mother! Please tell me this is good news!*

Did you pray as some mothers do: I hope I am up to being a mother. Please God, help me to be a good enough mother. I hope the baby and I will respond well to each other. Help us to teach our baby about you, about love, about your presence in all of life. Help us to be love and presence to our baby.

Mary, you were so young. What understanding did you have of yourself at that time? How can I relate with you mother of Jesus?

Mary, would you say 'yes' again?

Revelation

> *When it's over … I don't want to find myself sighing and frightened, or full of argument.*[5]

Mary, in everything, you know that God is present. In your thoughts and desires, your hopes and disappointments, and your actions, God is with you.

You think a great deal about Joseph; about how special he is to your family, and how he will be your husband soon. You wonder what it will be like to be a wife but you trust your parents with the marriage arrangement. Joseph is a man of honour, sincerity and humour. You believe he is the answer to your family's prayer.

As you contemplate your future, wondering about the wedding celebration, you are touched with overwhelming gratitude to God. You take off your shoes and feel the soles of your feet make cool contact with the earth. Years of treading and sweeping have firmed and smoothed the surface. You know that soon you will walk on Joseph's crafted floors.

You notice a curious luminescence around you. You hear a voice which initially alarms you. You retreat.

"Do not be afraid."

You are calmed by the words in your heart.

You reply, "I am listening."

Still and peaceful now, aware that the voice is familiar, you hear a clear message which signifies a turning point for you. It is both far-reaching and deeply personal.

You ask: "How can this be?"

And even as you ask, you know to put your trust in God's complete trustworthiness. You are open to God. Nothing more is necessary. You cannot help but say 'yes' to God. You cannot help but say 'yes' to God's word made real through your response to Mystery.

In Mary's Heart – 1

God of love, I know you are speaking to me. The knowledge and gift of your greatness in the face of my smallness is weighty. I love you God. The more I give you my love the more you bless me.

But today you ask something important of me!

I want to stay here. Your touch stills me. I am aware that my body is holy. Your life is in the breath I breathe. I say 'yes' to you. I cannot imagine a thought without you.

May your word to me be fulfilled.

Reflect and Respond

Is there something God asks of you?

In Grace ...

God waits.

Mary prays.

Her veil falls.

*At this moment
there is no fear,
even though she does not know
the outcome of her bearing
towards God.*

*Her heart whispers yes
to God-with-her,*

*yes,
compelling love.*

In You God

*I am
vulnerable and strong
in you God, I am
trusting and awe-filled
in you God, I am
empty and certain
in you
God
I am.*

Mary Visits Elizabeth

At that time Mary got ready and hurried to a town in the hill country of Judea, where she entered Zechariah's home and greeted Elizabeth. When Elizabeth heard Mary's greeting, the baby leaped in her womb, and Elizabeth was filled with the Holy Spirit. In a loud voice she exclaimed: "Blessed are you among women, and blessed is the child you will bear! But why am I so favoured, that the mother of my Lord should come to me? ... Mary stayed with Elizabeth for about three months and then returned home. (Lk1:39-43,56).

Magnificat

My soul glorifies the Lord and my spirit rejoices in God my Savior, for he has been mindful of the humble state of his servant. From now on all generations will call me blessed, for the Mighty One has done great things for me — holy is his name. His mercy extends to those who fear him, from generation to generation. He has performed mighty deeds with his arm; he has scattered those who are proud in their inmost thoughts. He has brought down rulers from their thrones but has lifted up the humble. He has filled the hungry with good things but has sent the rich away empty. He has helped his servant Israel, remembering to be merciful to Abraham and his descendants forever, just as he promised our ancestors. (Lk1:46-55, see also 1Sam1:11; 2:1-10; Ps111:9; 98:3; 107:9; Isa41:8-9).

Mary Speaks to Elizabeth

Let your religion be less of a theory and more of a love affair.[6]

Elizabeth! I am so happy to see you. I wish I could have come sooner, but I have not been up to the travel. How are you? The baby is beginning to look heavy. This is good, yes? I have a parcel of baby clothes for you. I made them myself. And when you have finished with them, you can pass them back to me!

What is this? Thank you. Woven by you? It is perfect Elizabeth. I shall treasure it. In fact, I will use it the day our baby is born. I am beginning to be excited now. And you; I am so excited for you. This is a dream come true. Let me hug you. Let me be close to this baby and to you.

'We have so much to talk about. Thank you for this special friendship. I trust you Elizabeth with my deepest thoughts.

'Tell me, how is Zechariah going? I trust he will be restored to full health once the baby is delivered. It has been quite a series of events for him. In fact for all of the family!

'I pray to God every day for you. And I am moved as I thank God for everything and especially for you'.

Reflect and Respond

'The Almighty has done great things for me'.

You might like to write your own Magnificat.

I Hope

my heart is big enough
to tend my baby's cry

my hands open enough
to hold and free the reins

my mind clear enough
to remember God's mercy

my words few enough
to allow God space

The Birth of Jesus

And she gave birth to her firstborn, a son. She wrapped him in cloths and placed him in a manger, because there was no guest room available for them. And there were shepherds living out in the fields nearby, keeping watch over their flocks at night. An angel of the Lord appeared to them, and the glory of the Lord shone around them, and they were terrified. But the angel said to them, "Do not be afraid. I bring you good news that will cause great joy for all the people. Today in the town of David a Savior has been born to you; he is the Messiah, the Lord. This will be a sign to you: you will find a baby wrapped in cloths and lying in a manger." Suddenly a great company of the heavenly host appeared with the angel, praising God and saying, "Glory to God in the highest heaven, and on earth peace to those on whom his favor rests."

So they hurried off and found Mary and Joseph, and the baby, who was lying in the manger. (Lk2:7-14,16; see also Lk2:15,17-20; The Visit of the Magi – Mt2:1-12).

Hosanna Lullaby

Joseph is outside. He observes the approach of the shepherds and is apprehensive until they tell him what was revealed to them. Their story is a gift to Joseph. It assures him of God's faithfulness. The shepherds also are confirmed that God's word can be trusted.

Joseph asks for the guest room but, under the busy circumstances, only the lower quarters of the house are available. Mary and Joseph are housed close to the animals which come in to shelter there at night.

Joseph bends down close to Mary. He tells her the shepherds' story. Mary is amazed. Quietly, the shepherds come inside. Joseph asks if they would like to hold Jesus.

A young shepherdess lifts him onto her shoulder. She gently rocks him back and forth as she hums a lullaby. Jesus' tiny body molds into her shape. She says he is warm and wonderful. She does not want to let him go.

In Mary's Heart – 2

God, I am so thankful everything has gone well. Though it is unusual, I am especially thankful that Joseph was there to help with the delivery. When I am strong, we will celebrate. We will make the journey to see Elizabeth and Zechariah and share a special meal with them.

I am excited, tired and happy. God, please help me to sleep peacefully, for I expect to be woken again quite soon. Thank you for the miraculous gift of a son. He is beyond all our hopes. You are the source of all life, all joy.

Reflect and Respond

Imagine the joy which Jesus brought to Mary and Joseph. Imagine the joy which Mary and Joseph brought to Jesus. Who has brought joy to your life? To whom have you brought joy?

According to Joseph

As a carpenter, I love outdoors –
the smells of animals and hay.
I am drawn to rough and cluttered sheds.
I shape and whittle undressed wood
until smooth as newborn skin.

I was in Bethlehem to register for taxes.
Mary wanted to come with me
though it seemed unwise.
That's how I became the 'midwife' –
a not-yet-husband, teary and helping
to bring our baby into the world
into an environment I love.

There are stories told but
for all I know, the whole world
might have been a choir.
I wouldn't have heard them –
I sobbed so much.

Sealed

in homage to the carpenter's son, three wooden boxes cloaked in purple cloth, come from the gifting magi. In the darkness, Mary removes the bunch

of cloth. With delight, she smells the sudden drift of cedar, strokes the smoothness, recognizes a patient hand. She smiles at Joseph. He holds one box

by candlelight, sees it glimmer, admires its proportion and aesthetics. Over time, they open them; the gifts that Jesus has to celebrate and share

Jesus Is Presented to God

And when the time came for the purification rites required by the Law of Moses, Joseph and Mary took [Jesus] to Jerusalem to present him to the Lord: *Every first-born male must be consecrated to the Lord.*

Now there was a man in Jerusalem called Simeon, who was righteous and devout. He was waiting for the consolation of Israel, and the Holy Spirit was on him. It had been revealed to him by the Holy Spirit that he would not die before he had seen the Lord's Messiah. Moved by the Spirit, he went into the temple courts. When the parents brought in the child Jesus to do for him what the custom of the Law required, Simeon took him in his arms and praised God, saying: "Sovereign Lord, as you have promised, you may now dismiss your servant in peace. For my eyes have seen your salvation, which you have prepared in the sight of all nations: a light for revelation to the Gentiles, and the glory of your people Israel." The child's father and mother marveled at what was said about him. Then Simeon blessed them and said to Mary, his mother: "This child is destined to cause the falling and rising of many in Israel, and to be a sign that will be spoken against, so that the thoughts of many hearts will be revealed. And a sword will pierce your own soul too."

There was also a prophet, Anna. She had lived with her husband seven years after her marriage, and then was a widow until she was eighty-four. She never left the temple but worshiped night and day, fasting and praying. Coming up to them at that very moment, she gave thanks to God and spoke about the child to all who were looking forward to the redemption of Jerusalem. (Lk 2:22, 23b, 25-36a, 37-38; see also Ex 13:2).

The Seer

Mary and Joseph carry Jesus to the Temple. Simeon is waiting for them. This is an important and solemn day. The mother is to be purified. The child is to be dedicated. Joseph gives Jesus to Simeon who lifts him before God in an act of consecration. Simeon, wise and prayerful, sees beyond present realities to possibilities. He sees who Jesus is because he sees who Jesus can be. As they dedicate Jesus to God, Simeon is humbled by the faithful obedience of Mary and Joseph. As he kneels before God, he is also aware that he kneels before a holy family.

In Mary's Heart – 3

There is so much being said about Jesus. I am beginning to be overwhelmed. I am an ordinary girl. I do not have any special insights about being a mother or about educating Jesus in the Jewish laws and practices. You must have wanted an ordinary home for Jesus because that is what Joseph and I can offer. We will do our best, and try to be diligent in prayer and worship.

It is difficult to imagine the lofty potential which Anna spoke about today. We shall have to go quietly through the tasks of our daily lives, remaining close to you God, for it is clear that we will need your peaceful presence.

Reflect and Respond

What acts of consecration do you recognize in your life history?

Remember a time when God spoke to you through a modern-day prophet or friend.

Summoned

mother
hears baby's tiny
cry
trumpet
in the night
Eyes shut
she lifts   the covers
and herself
runs fingers
along the wall
makes each step
creak   comfort to
baby's   side

This   child
she   knows
has   saved
her   from
her   self

Mary and Joseph Find Jesus in the Temple

When he was twelve years old, they went up to the festival, according to the custom. After the festival was over, while his parents were returning home, the boy Jesus stayed behind in Jerusalem, but they were unaware of it. Thinking he was in their company, they travelled on for a day. Then they began looking for him among their relatives and friends. When they did not find him, they went back to Jerusalem to look for him. After three days they found him in the temple courts, sitting among the teachers, listening to them and asking them questions. Everyone who heard him was amazed at his understanding and his answers. When his parents saw him, they were astonished. His mother said to him, "Son, why have you treated us like this? Your father and I have been anxiously searching for you." "Why were you searching for me?" he asked. "Didn't you know I had to be in my Father's house?" But they did not understand what he was saying to them. (Lk2:42-50).

The Scenario

If this be lost, let us be lost always.[7]

The child Jesus was consecrated to God twelve years before this incident in the Temple. In this part of the Gospel, Jesus lives out that consecration. His parents do not readily make this connection that all their formative work in the traditional ways and wisdom of Judaism has come to fruit in this moment.

Mary and Joseph are distressed when they realize that Jesus is missing. In fact he is missing for three days. Were these 'three days' stressful for Jesus too? The temptation to self-doubt lurks in new situations, and here, especially as night fell, Jesus might have keenly felt the absence of his parents.

Luke, the gospel evangelist, is setting the stage to show the nature of Jesus' relationship with God; Jesus has his mind and heart on God, and he does not compromise.

When Jesus' parents find him in the Temple, there is no sentimental reunion. Jesus speaks the facts to Mary and Joseph as though surprised that they could be worried by his absence. 'Did you not know that I must be busy with my Father's affairs?'

We understand the concerns of Mary and Joseph. If we listen carefully, we might understand Jesus' surprise, because he was embodying what his parents taught him about putting God first in his life. Jesus was at the age when he was to make his 'adult' commitment to God.

Mary and Joseph are astounded by the sincerity and zeal which Jesus displays. They think of Jesus as a boy, not a man. In their view, he ought to be obedient to them. They do not understand the question he puts to them.

Here is an opportunity for Mary and Joseph to re-present him and re-consecrate Jesus to the care of God.

In Mary's Heart – 4

I am worried. We cannot find Jesus anywhere. We must go to the Temple to plead for Jesus and ourselves.

***

Now that we have found him, we are relieved and angry. Joseph is silent. He is choked with fear about what he might do. Can Jesus not grasp the meaning of what he has done? Clearly he has something else on his mind. Joseph and I are confounded by his response! God, I have prayed that you will make my heart larger. Now I am beginning to know what that involves. I am certain of one thing: it is only in your grace that I can do what you ask of me.

***

Thank you for reuniting us with Jesus. I am reminded of my own childhood. Help me to love the child within myself.

Reflect and Respond

Presenting ourselves before God is an act of surrender to the unfolding mystery of grace, regardless of how we feel about the events or circumstances of our lives. We are free when our deep desires are one with God. At such times, we reflect God.

Consider the friendship of worry, trust; suffering, joy.

That Day

She said yes
not knowing how
         she discovered
motherhood
was not a fantasy

She said yes
not knowing

         how
much she would try
to bear his struggles
to fathom the descent
to lonely places where
he went
         and found
truth and desire merge

         At times she knew

loss and gain
as one
intense love,

when she would have said yes
again.

Light

When I am among trees …
The light flows from their branches…
and you too have come into the world to do this.[8]
— Mary Oliver

Jesus Is Baptized

At that time Jesus came from Nazareth in Galilee and was baptized by John in the Jordan. Just as Jesus was coming up out of the water, he saw heaven being torn open and the Spirit descending on him like a dove. And a voice came from heaven: "you are my Son, whom I love; with you I am well pleased." (Mk1:9-11, see also Mt3:13-17; Lk3:21-23a; Jn1:32-34).

River Jordan

> *If you are capable of living deeply one moment of your life, you can learn to live the same way all other moments of your life.*[9]

Jesus sits quietly on the banks of the river Jordan. For days, he has watched his charismatic cousin John urging people to repent. Jesus has always admired John for challenging societal norms. This has been costly for John.

Today, drawn and consoled, Jesus responds to John's invitation. Jesus wants to identify with others who publicly commit themselves to God. For Jesus, baptism is a declaration of God calling him into public ministry. He knows it will be costly for him.

From the river shallows, John sees Jesus walk down to the water's edge. He watches him remove his sandals and outer garment then wade into the cool water. John feels humbled in the presence of Jesus. He is insisting that Jesus baptize him instead. But Jesus insists that John baptize him.

Jesus sinks down into the water and comes up again. In the bright light of the day, people cannot see clearly what is happening. Some think they can see a lone dove in the sky above Jesus. Others claim that they hear a voice from the heavens 'you are my Son, the Beloved. In you, I am well pleased'.

Most people go home thinking that a trick has been played on them. Some discuss with their friends what they saw happen in the Jordan that day. They are curious about the man Jesus.

Many of John's disciples recognize the power of that moment and want to follow Jesus instead of John. They are the first of many who feel drawn to him.

After the baptism, Jesus continues to experience a heightened awareness of God with him. He is conscious of the solemn reality of his calling. He communes with God, consoled by God's abiding Presence.

In Mary's Heart – 5

Gracious God, each of the last few days Jesus has gone to the Jordan river where John urges people to repent of their sins and be baptized. John has been faithful to what he understands is his calling. He is an Essene. I know membership of this sect is not for the faint-hearted. Its values are consistent with those Jesus has incorporated into his life.

I know that Jesus will be baptized. He seems to feel the need to do what many sincere and passionate people do. He says that he believes in solidarity with the poor and with people on the fringes of society. I need to follow him today, God. This seems the thing to do though I am not sure why.

When I look for him, I find that he is in the river preparing to be baptized. He has gone under the water. Now as he comes up, I am caught by his appearance. There is a bird hovering above him. I hear a voice come from somewhere; the words so clearly fixed in my mind: 'you are my Son, the beloved; and with you I am pleased'.

He is your child, your son, loving father and mother God. Sometimes I forget that this is so. But today, I present him to you again and relinquish any contrary wants in favor of your loving desire. I am praying because I need to. I need to feel your peace.

You are gracious God in helping me let go of Jesus now he is a man. I want to live within you God. You are my strength. Lead me beside gentle waters when my instincts want Jesus back home. I am in awe of your grace. I love and praise you God for the favors granted to Joseph, Jesus and me. You are always there.

Reflect and Respond

Listen to God. When have you sensed God's pleasure in you? Can you imagine God say to you, 'you are my child, beloved; and with you I am well pleased'?

The Best Wine

A wedding took place at Cana in Galilee. Jesus' mother was there, and Jesus and his disciples had also been invited to the wedding. When the wine was gone, Jesus' mother said to him, "They have no more wine." "Woman, why do you involve me?" Jesus replied. "My hour has not yet come." His mother said to the servants, "Do whatever he tells you."

Nearby stood six stone water jars, the kind used by the Jews for ceremonial washing, each holding from twenty to thirty gallons. Jesus said to the servants, "Fill the jars with water"; so they filled them to the brim. Then he told them, "Now draw some out and take it to the master of the banquet." They did so, and the master of the banquet tasted the water that had been turned into wine. He did not realize where it had come from, though the servants who had drawn the water knew. Then he called the bridegroom aside and said, "Everyone brings out the choice wine first and then the cheaper wine after the guests have had too much to drink; but you have saved the best till now."

What Jesus did here in Cana of Galilee was the first of the signs through which he revealed his glory; and his disciples believed in him. After this he went down to Capernaum with his mother and brothers and his disciples. There they stayed for a few days. (Jn2:1-12).

The Meaning of the Miracle

> *What if the world is holding its breath — waiting for you to take the place that only you can fill?* [10]

A feast is the chosen place for the public revelation of Jesus' identity. A marriage feast is significant in that it celebrates something of the love possible between two people and between God and people. The miracle narrative is rich in symbols: the changing of water, symbolic of life itself, into wine, a symbol of joy and hope. In the light of the whole Gospel, this miracle sets the scene for the importance which John the evangelist gives to 'drinking' the living water Jesus gives.

Jesus' reply to his mother seems, in our contemporary culture, brisk and surprising. As Luke demonstrated in the story of the Finding of the Child Jesus in the Temple, John draws a distinction between the importance for Jesus of doing God's will and doing the will of Mary, his mother. In this story, Mary also acts upon what she experiences as God's will. As it happens, Mary is able to take the lead. She demonstrates that she trusts the goodness of Jesus.

Why does Jesus perform the miracle if his 'hour has not come yet'? It could be that John is alluding to what we might theologically name, the not yet dimension of the fullness of God in creation. But Jesus shows that it is possible to celebrate now because he is the present revelation of God's love.

This is cause for the best wine.

In Mary's Heart – 6

God, I know now that I did the right thing in mentioning the bride and bridegroom's dilemma to Jesus. The poor couple! How embarrassed the families and guests might have been! At first Jesus was reluctant to help but he did not take long to discern what to do.

It can be difficult being a mother of adult children. I find it hard to know when to speak and when not to speak to Jesus. He seems preoccupied with his thoughts at times. Sometimes he doesn't seem to hear me.

I am not sure but it seemed that he distanced himself from me today. I felt it sharply.

But now, as I speak, I am assured that Jesus' mind and heart are in you. He wants me to know that, and mostly I do, but sometimes it gets the better of me and I want him to be my little boy again.

I was thankful when I saw Jesus go over to the servants. I didn't hear what was said, so I was surprised when our cups were full of wine again. It was strange that I felt the urge to speak to the servants. Normally I would not do that, especially as a guest at a wedding. I thought extra wine might be brought from elsewhere. I am stunned that Jesus changed his mind so quickly and with such grace.

Somehow I feel changed myself.

Praise be to you my God for helping me to trust myself and Jesus' kind benevolence.

Imaginative Contemplation

Today was Yohan and Hada's long awaited day. Family and friends gathered for the wedding. They danced and sang, told stories about the couple, about their obvious love – a marriage written in their hearts.

Just before the meal was served, Mary whispered to Jesus, *They have no wine.*

Jesus replied, *Yohan and Hada don't seem worried. Why are you worried?*

But Mary knew the embarrassment this oversight was to the family. Wine is the symbol of joy and hospitality. It is warmth and celebration. And there was none left!

After his conversation with Mary, Jesus went outside alone. The music gave way to the bleat of sheep. Jesus smelt the scent of cut grass in the spring air. From an untidy grapevine growing along an old fence, he picked an immature grape and pressed it. The pungent smell made him feel sad.

He was pleased that he had been invited to propose the toast to the wedding couple. He rehearsed his planned speech. Then he decided to say something different. He returned to the celebration.

Yohan and Hada, your many gifts are magnified through sharing them. Hold each other in love and with open hands. Let us stand to drink. Let us pray that love makes wine of water.

Reflect and Respond

How do you know when to speak and when to be silent?

When have you been surprised by God?

The Good News

After John was put in prison, Jesus went into Galilee, proclaiming the good news of God. "The time has come," he said. "The kingdom of God has come near. Repent and believe the good news!" … As Jesus walked beside the Sea of Galilee, he saw Simon and his brother Andrew casting a net into the lake, for they were fishermen. "Come, follow me," Jesus said, "and I will send you out to fish for people." At once they left their nets and followed him. When he had gone a little farther, he saw James son of Zebedee and his brother John in a boat, preparing their nets. Without delay he called them, and they left their father Zebedee in the boat with the hired men and followed him. (Mk1:14-20. See also Mt4:18-22; Lk5:1-11; Jn1:40-51).

The Time to Believe

Mark's narrative is told at an urgent pace. The reader hears the time to believe the good news is now. This is Jesus' call to the fishermen and to us. What does it mean? We can be sure that the fishermen did not know what it meant. They were intrigued by Jesus. They left what they were doing at that moment, later discovering what he meant by 'I will make you fishers of men'.

Once we decide to follow we cannot continue with our lives as they were. Jesus calls us to make changes. If we follow Jesus we discern and discover what those changes might be. Trusting Jesus is a choice. Trusting the good to which we are drawn is, at the same time, trusting ourselves.

The good news is that we are on a journey of love, one in which we will be truly free by following Christ within us. We do not have to wait a moment longer to live in abundant love and authentic freedom.

In Mary's Heart – 7

Please God, listen to the prayers of your children. John has been arrested! Help our family to stay close to each other and to you while John faces this ordeal.

Apart from this large challenge to our family, there are other challenges. Jesus says that I am bothered by small things. But I am tired and concerned about having enough money for food. Jesus brings strangers home to eat. Some stay for days while he teaches them. He is a great story-teller, but stories do not put food on the table. I am not sure what Jesus means when he says that the Kingdom of God is near.

Jesus knows I am tired. He looks tired himself. When we catch a few moments together, he tells me that it will be alright; that you, God will strengthen us and will provide the food we need.

Some of the fishermen's wives have gathered to listen to Jesus as well. I have developed friendships with a few of them. And they help me cook the fish.

This is all new to me. My life changes every day. Thank you for my friends. Thank you for my relatives. I trust you God for your provision and your faithfulness to me. Thank you for teaching me through Jesus to trust you moment by moment.

Please make it possible for me to visit Elizabeth again very soon. I wait on your timing, my God.

Reflect and Respond

Jesus speaks to you, 'Follow me'. What questions do you have?

Living Water

Jesus answered [the Samaritan woman], "If you knew the gift of God and who it is that asks you for a drink, you would have asked him and he would have given you living water." (Jn4:10; see also Jn4:1-30; 39-42).

The Gift of God

Who is this Jesus?

Jesus does not expect the Samaritan woman to know him or to understand God's offer. (Later in the gospel, the disciples on the road to Emmaus struggled to *recognize* Jesus, let alone *know* him.)

Is it possible that the Samaritan woman begins her journey with Jesus after meeting him at Jacob's well? The unusual nature of their exchange intrigues and challenges her. The fact that she returns to her townsfolk to talk about Jesus, and that many people believe on the strength of her words, indicates that something is changing in her life.

The Samaritan woman seeks more than water. She longs for the living water to refresh her, make her well and fully alive.

The offer of living water moves and challenges us today. May we come to know the one who offers us this life-changing gift.

In Mary's Heart – 8

God of my ancestors, my friend Sarai saw Jesus with a foreign woman at Jacob's well yesterday. The synagogue authorities will not be pleased. Last night, I cautioned Jesus for his sake and for the sake of the woman. I reminded him that Samaritans have standards too.

Jesus reminded me about the circumstances of his birth. He smiled and said that I have been no example in terms of holding fast to custom.

Of course he speaks the truth. Always. Yet I am worried that he is drawing too much attention to himself. Is there a way that he can act in accord with your desires God without upsetting the authorities?

Reflect and Respond

How have you or others you know experienced the cost of discipleship?

Christ the Light

After six days Jesus took with him Peter, James and John, the brother of James, and led them up a high mountain by themselves. There he was transfigured before them. His face shone like the sun, and his clothes became as white as the light. Just then there appeared before them Moses and Elijah, talking with Jesus. Peter said to Jesus, "Lord, it is good for us to be here. If you wish, I will put up three shelters—one for you, one for Moses and one for Elijah." While he was still speaking, a bright cloud covered them, and a voice from the cloud said, "This is my Son, whom I love; with him I am well pleased. Listen to him!" When the disciples heard this, they fell facedown to the ground, terrified. But Jesus came and touched them. "Get up," he said. "Don't be afraid." When they looked up, they saw no one except Jesus. As they were coming down the mountain, Jesus instructed them, "Don't tell anyone what you have seen until the Son of Man has been raised from the dead." (Mt17:1-9. See also Mk9:2-8; Lk9:28-36).

Touched

> *The mystic allows one thing to be mysterious, and everything else becomes lucid.*[11]

Symbols such as high mountain, bright cloud and tents indicate places of meeting between God and those present. The presence of Moses and Elijah points to the anointed role of prophet and seer which is integral to Jesus' ministry. Jesus is transfigured - 'his face shone like the sun, and his clothes became white as the light'. Peter experiences this as an inspirational moment. He is moved to respond, and does so with the extravagant suggestion that he honour the moment with the construction of three shelters or shrines of dedication.

Jesus noticeably does not reply at this point. Instead, Peter, James and John hear a voice which stills them when they cannot still themselves. The voice attests to God's intimate relationship with Jesus.

Peter, James and John are terrified. They find peaceful relief only when Jesus touches them and says, 'do not be afraid'. These are the same words Mary heard when she was called to be the mother of Jesus.

In Mary's Heart – 9

I miss seeing Jesus as often as I once did. He is busy teaching in the synagogues and visiting the sick. I know he yearns for some quiet time and space in the evenings.

He loses himself in that time of communion with you. Sometimes it is as though I am looking at an angel. His eyes are deep and yet they hide nothing from me. He shares all he has with me, all he knows.

When he appears almost luminous in prayer, I am reminded we need a 'light' in our too-often dark world.

Jesus is many things to me. He encourages me when I am afraid or anxious. He holds me when I am lonely. His presence is enough to calm me. If only everyone could know him as I do. I trust him and know that he is your son, my God. I praise you every day for bringing him into my life.

Though I feel unworthy of your constant attention to me, I know that your love is always around and within me.

Reflect and Respond

What is your experience of Jesus in relationship to you?

Who Is My Mother?

While Jesus was still talking to the crowd, his mother and brothers stood outside, wanting to speak to him. Someone told him, "Your mother and brothers are standing outside, wanting to speak to you." He replied to him, "Who is my mother, and who are my brothers?" Pointing to his disciples, he said, "Here are my mother and my brothers. For whoever does the will of my Father in heaven is my brother and sister and mother." (Mt12:46-50 also Lk8:19-21 and Mk3:31-35).

Communion in Love

The family of Jesus is larger than his blood relatives. Jesus wants to be our brother, sharing the same community of people who love God and seek to discern and enact their unique pathway in the world. This is the graced pathway which contributes most fully to individual, communal and universal wholeness.

In Mary's Heart – 10

I notice that Jesus' visits are further apart these days and he is collecting many followers. The crowds stopped me from seeing him today. Am I to wait outside the synagogue so that I can see my son? Jesus has told me that all these people are his family. I understand what he means to some extent. They love him and want to follow his teaching. They are drawing more closely to you God. This is of course a good thing. I am also aware that there are people who do not like Jesus and his teaching. I suspect this might be dangerous for him.

Reflect and Respond

What do you understand by 'the will of God' in our contemporary world?

Unclenched

I pray you might

... slacken my jaw
        to sing praises

... unhunch my back
        to sit honorably

... unfrown my eyes
        to smile truly

... unpurse my lips
        to speak gently

... slow my steps
        to dance freely

... relinquish my fear
        to hope expansively

... unclutter my brain
        to ponder silently

... liberate my heart
        to love abundantly.

*We are here to be part of the great song
and we don't even have to know the song,
we just have to know our note.*[12]
— Rumi

Body of Christ

When the hour came, Jesus and his apostles reclined at the table. And he said to them, "I have eagerly desired to eat this Passover with you before I suffer. For I tell you, I will not eat it again until it finds fufilment in the kingdom of God." After taking the cup, he gave thanks and said, "Take this and divide it among you. For I tell you I will not drink again from the fruit of the vine until the kingdom of God comes." And he took bread, gave thanks and broke it, and gave it to them, saying, "This is my body given for you; do this in remembrance of me." In the same way, after the supper he took the cup, saying, "This cup is the new covenant in my blood, which is poured out for you. (Lk22:14-20. See also Mt26:26-30; Mk14:22-25).

Eucharist as Gift

Jesus loves the traditional Passover meal because it recalls much that is precious in the history of the Jewish people.

This night he adds a new dimension to the Passover narratives. Jesus becomes part of the story. We bring to life the reality of his life, death and resurrection as we share in breaking bread and drinking from the cup.

In Mary's Heart – 11

God, though I know I am in you and you in me, I am merely going through the motions of recalling the Passover. I cannot feel too much about it at all. This room is not the one where we gather usually. It is quite dark and even damp. I am glad I have my coat with me.

I am missing Joseph tonight. Even though he has been gone for some time, in my heart I hear his voice, his singing, his praising God in the psalms and I want him here beside me. As we spoke of the meaning of the bitter herbs, I turned to look for him, as if some strange hope possessed me.

Of course Joseph is here with me in many ways. He is here in Jesus. Sometimes I notice the way Jesus tilts his head or smiles or uses certain phrases, then I see my dearest Joseph. I know I am so very Jewish in this way — memories are present as I remember them.

Jesus has many friends sharing the meal with him — men and women who have been faithful to him. In fact, it is quite crowded in the room. Nobody minds because it is warmer that way. Being close to others is what Passover is all about — we celebrate who we are as a people with a strong history and a strong future in God.

As I write these thoughts, my spirits are lifting. Mary from Magdala smiles at me across the table. She has an uncanny sense of reading my heart, and she communicates love and joy without words. I have grown to like her a great deal. She is a good friend to Jesus, and I suspect she is a confidante as well.

One thing about tonight has confused me. What did Jesus mean when he said that the bread we shared was his body? And he said something about the wine being his blood. This is reminiscent of the blood of the lamb smeared on the doorposts in Egypt. The blood enabled freedom to our Jewish forebears. Jesus talks in dense language. It both frightens and consoles me.

My God, I am an ordinary woman but my life has been extraordinary. It is over thirty years since your promise came to me. Still I am astounded by your calling. Still I ask why me, my God?

And you begin to speak to me so quietly and gently . . .

Why not, Mary, my love?

Reflect and Respond

In what ways do you share eucharist?

We Come ...

expecting
to remember, and
make truly present
his body
and ours
broken
each for the other
healed
by the other.

This Bread

Come, share this bread with me
my eternal meal
which gives meaning to all meals.
Sit a while with me.
Know what you are doing here.
I am sharing this time with you,
longing to etch in your mind
a lasting memory. Taste the wine.
Remember its bitter-sweetness for all time.
Remember the touch of our fingers
as I pass the cup to you;
how our eyes are drawn to each other
just being together,
forgetting all else for this moment.

***

How could I have understood the suffering
we would endure for the sake of each other?

Jesus, did you know the cost of saying 'yes'?

Each time I ponder your life,
I see its end, the most vindictive death of all.

>Eradicate him.
>Can't have mind polluters
>with visions of power and a kingdom
>competing with our own.
>Do away with him.

*And again I ponder your life.
I am filled with emotion, with your love.
I am taken out of myself,
see myself as I am,
hear a call upon my mind, my heart, my hands.
Grace spills into my
ordinariness.*

*I recall my adolescent 'yes'
when I was yet to know its cost.
I think of the cross,
smell the air warm with your
                              struggling breath.
I taste the bread of our closeness
       and I can barely lift the cup
in my sorrow, my grief.*

My heart is not big enough for such love.

*I shut my eyes.
My mind is opened
by the poetry of your risen life.
Into my wounded-ness, your spirit comes
to heal and swell my heart.*

Listen ... I Am

just like you
chosen for a heavy task —
to carry precious cargo
along the streets
of Jerusalem.

O holy city, wholly
I hear your voice
in my ear, so gentle, all
I am
is lost
in one sense.

A colt is what I am.
I led your voice
to the kiss
of Gethsemane.

Still
I can hear you.

Suffering

*Tell your heart that the fear of suffering is worse than the suffering itself.
And that no heart has ever suffered when it goes in search of its dreams,
because every second of the search is a second's encounter
with God and with eternity.*[13]
— Paul Coelho

Decision in the Garden

Jesus went out as usual to the Mount of Olives, and his disciples followed him. On reaching the place, he said to them, "Pray that you will not fall into temptation." He withdrew about a stone's throw beyond them, knelt down and prayed, "Father, if you are willing, take this cup from me; yet not my will, but yours be done."

An angel from heaven appeared to him and strengthened him. And being in anguish, he prayed more earnestly, and his sweat was like drops of blood falling to the ground. (Lk22:39-44. See also Mt 26:36-41; Mk14:35).

In Mary's Heart – 12

Almighty God, you are with Jesus. He has prayed a great deal lately. He is seeking guidance. At times I have watched him break out in a fretful sweat as though there is dread in him. Later he tells me that I need not fear for God is accompanying him.

Jesus promises to be with me forever. How can he be with me forever. No-one except you, God, can do that. I have heard him say this to the crowds who follow him. The Jewish officials will not be pleased.

There was an oppressive air tonight, not so much at the Seder, but later, in the night, I sensed that something was wrong. Earlier today, my friends stopped talking when I joined them. It was as if they had been talking about Jesus or me. Many things are flashing through my mind. God, please make sense of them for me. God, have mercy on me. Be my strength.

No! Word has come that soldiers have arrested Jesus and taken him away.

What do they think he has done? He is a good son. People love him. He has compassion for anyone who suffers. What is happening? What charges could they be concocting? If only I had listened to my heart about Judas. Give Jesus courage and a strong sense of himself. Help him to be faithful to you and to this test of faithfulness.

Perhaps this nightmare will end very soon. Jesus will be back to tell me that it had all been a mistake and that we will travel back to Galilee in a few days. It is so difficult not knowing. I cannot rest until I know that he is safe. God, I know that you have not abandoned Jesus. Show me this is true.

Before you and with you God, I am praying humbly.

Reflect and Respond

Think about fear, confusion, and their opposites love and trust. What parts do they play in your life?

Oh Judas

      you will do anything
for money
  even betrayal of a friend

what
  seized your mind
 judas
      you won't look at Jesus
       you kiss him instead
  your mind
    on lowly things
could not imagine
    what would ensue.
 you did it
         for money
  judas

you cannot sleep
     for guilt and sorrow
       for hatred of yourself
     and them

  you throw down your silver, yourself

to

death

  oh judas we needed you

you could have wept for love

Are You a King?

Pilate, do you question all suspected criminals?

      Where are you from?
      What is truth?
      Are you king of the Jews?

Whose questions are these?

Do you know
you cannot speak with Jesus
and be the same again?

This is your moment of unbearable truth.

Can you listen?
Your heart knows the truth.
Listen to the insight of the woman.

Fear mocks you.

I find no fault   reverberates
through your whole being

Thirty times

you scourge yourself.

Jesus Is Flogged

Pilate announced to the chief priests and the crowd, "I find no basis for a charge against this man. ...

Neither has Herod, for he sent him back to us; as you can see, he has done nothing to deserve death. Therefore, I will punish him and then release him. (Lk23:4,16)

Then Pilate took Jesus and had him flogged. (Jn19:1. See also Isa53:3-8).

Scourged and Despised

You can only find truth with logic if you have already found truth without it.[14]

Pilate points his finger at the chest of Jesus. He wants Jesus to know that if he doesn't make a good account of himself, it will be the death of him. Jesus stands silently. It is as if the scenario is happening in slow motion. The silence is deafening to those who love Jesus.

Jesus will not compromise. That is one of his great strengths. Some might call him stubborn, but no-one knows better than his mother that Jesus is not stubborn.

Jesus has a conviction deeper than anyone about what is truth. That is why so many of his disciples are running away. They know that Jesus will not give in to the pressure of the scribes and elders who want him to obey the exacting Jewish law.

The Romans cannot possibly understand that Jesus wants only to follow the path which is ordained for him. Pilate and Herod think of Jesus as a harmless madman. They misunderstand the power which many of the Jewish leaders invest in preserving the status quo. Jesus is a threat to the law they guard so closely.

There are few who stand by Jesus. Mary, his mother, refuses to leave him. She has to be restrained when the soldiers deliver that first lash. We watch her body recoil as if she receives the scourging herself. She cries out until she is silent too.

In Mary's Heart – 13

Merciful God, I cannot bear to watch my Jesus flogged. And I cannot bear to turn away. There is nowhere to turn but to you, God. This is a wicked hour for Jesus and for me. He is frail under the relentless torrent of flogging. I must bind his wounds. God, let me bind his wounds. Let him catch a glimpse of my eyes so that he will know I love him. God, why is this happening to him?

God, I cannot hear you.

Reflect and Respond

Can you think about a time when you or your loved ones were under unrelenting pressure? What enabled you to survive?

Jesus Is Crowned with Thorns

Then the soldiers of the governor took Jesus into the Praetorium and gathered the whole Roman cohort around Him. They stripped him and put a scarlet robe on him and then twisted together a crown of thorns and set it on his head. They put a staff in his right hand. Then they knelt in front of him and mocked him. "Hail, king of the Jews". (Mt27:27-29. See also Jn19:5, 16; Mk15:14).

Humiliated and Violated

The 'whole cohort'! What a testimony to the worst side of our nature is given in the passion narrative of Matthew's gospel. The whole cohort wanted to demean, deride and perpetrate evil on an innocent man. How much hatred is in their hearts this day!

It is painful to reflect upon the person, a servant or a soldier, who was commissioned to make a thorny crown to put on Jesus' head: of all the people in those governor's quarters, this person was the one who knew what suffering Jesus would endure for the sake of that evil commissioning. As he passed the crown of thorns, fresh with blood from his own hands, to one of the Roman soldiers, we can perhaps imagine that he felt compassion for Jesus. And Jesus, our servant, would have known the movements of the man's heart, and would have communicated the deepest knowledge of his love.

I am troubled that I am able to imagine so well the derision in which the whole cohort was engaged. I can imagine these people wanting Jesus to pose in kingly poses, to lift the laughable royal sceptre at just the right angle, to make him say royal phrases, and punish him for doing so. I am distraught that I understand evil so well and that it is this evil which caused the suffering of Jesus and his ultimate suffering, death.

Jesus, how hideous is evil.

In Mary's Heart – 14

What can I plead now, God in your heaven? You seem so far away from me. My son is being subjected to the most humiliating and painful of all sufferings. I am being pierced through and through.

I would rather die myself than let him go through this torment. The soldiers have pushed me away. They won't let me touch my son. Is there any way out of this?

Will he die so young? Is there anything I can do to stop this crime? Where is your angel now, my God? I am struggling to say 'yes' to this!

Be my strength my God.

Reflect and Respond

What difficult decision have you faced or are you facing? What conversation could you have with God about this decision?

The Cross

Wanting to satisfy the crowd, Pilate released Barabbas to them. He had Jesus flogged, and handed him over to be crucified. (Mk15.15)

Carrying his own cross, he went out to the place of the Skull (which in Aramaic is called Golgotha). (Jn19:17).

As the soldiers led him away, they seized Simon from Cyrene, who was on his way in from the country, and put the cross on him and made him carry it behind Jesus. A large number of people followed him, including women who mourned and wailed for him. Jesus turned and said to them, "Daughters of Jerusalem, do not weep for me; weep for yourselves and for your children. (Lk23:26-28).

The Way to Calvary

In less than twenty-four hours, Jesus has been arrested, tried by the Jewish Sanhedrin, interviewed by both Pilate and Herod, been accused of blasphemy, been ridiculed and slapped, flogged and mocked as 'King of the Jews'. He has been degraded against the heinous criminal Jesus Barabbas, and has been condemned while Barabbas has been released. Perhaps Barabbas found salvation in that gesture.

Jesus now finds himself on the way to his crucifixion. He is so weak from the flogging and abuse, that the soldiers compel a passer-by, Simon, a man from the region of Cyrene, to assist in carrying the cross. Is there not one person who can offer to help? What prevents them from being moved to pity Jesus? What fears possess them? What shame? What confusion?

One can barely imagine the pain Jesus endured in his flesh and spirit. Jesus must have felt alone. In choosing to go the way of Calvary, Jesus experienced the effects of the evil of human sinfulness in a personal and degrading suffering. In the fullness of his humanity, he also met spiritual temptation. On face value, Jesus' suffering and death is evil and confrontational. The gospels narrate that Jesus was abandoned by his friends. But was he abandoned by God? At the faith level, in the light of the belief in Jesus as God's self-revelation, the Cross stands as God's complete immersion into human suffering. As such, it is an act of the deepest and truest love. It is also an act of authentic freedom. Our redemption and therefore freedom is in knowing, experiencing and responding to love. We are to be united with Jesus in suffering.

As we reflect on the Cross, how could we help but feel sorrow for the evil inflicted upon Jesus? How could we help but be convicted of the evil in our own lives?

Mary Talks to Her Friend

Thank you my friend for being with me right now. I am sorry that I am leaning on you. I feel weak but I must be strong for my son.

Who is the strong man they have dragged from the crowd? They are forcing him to carry the cross on his shoulders. 'Leave me be!' he shouts.

Is there no-one who will take pity on my son?

The man has stopped protesting. Something has changed his attitude. Perhaps Jesus spoke to him.

Surely this is a bad dream. Everything has happened so fast. I cannot concentrate on anything. Is it true that it was only last night that we celebrated Pesach? And today …

Did I faint? Thank you for helping me. We must catch up to Jesus. I don't want him to feel alone. Quickly! I cannot see him; the crowd is so dense. I cannot see my son. I want to look into Jesus' eyes. I want to mouth the words 'I love you'.

I can't find anyone I know. … Jesus …

I want the whip of cords – the one Jesus made to scourge evil from the Temple. I would whip a path for Jesus to escape. Let me go.

I don't understand this. Evil is all around us. Why would anyone want to assault an innocent man?

Leave him alone … I beg you.

Reflect and Respond

Think about the two groups of people present in the scripture from Luke. The verbs might help –

took charge; seized; made (him);
followed; mourned; lamented.

Where are you in your imaginative contemplation of the narrative?

Earthed

I am falling.
Please don't catch me.
I am falling between heaven and earth.

Unless I fall,
trampled, cracked and split
open,
unless I lift my face, my eyes
to gaze on Jesus' face
on the way
to Golgotha,

how can I know anything
about belonging
and giving oneself
in friendship?

Earth
for a time, let me
merge in you.

The Carpenter

learned
his father's trade

hammered his thumbs

made tables and chairs
of wood and nails

wholly made them
with love

God

How long must I wait
for this suffering to end?

I stand and sit and pace
and don't know
what to do with myself.
There is no relief.
The wine is sour.

Jesus there, nailed, bleeding, shaking
in the cold, disease attacking
his body, weak and vulnerable to everything
to which I am vulnerable.

My son,
it is now I know
the faithfulness of 'yes'
It is a piercing sword.

From my heart, blood and water run.

You came into my life
I took the chance to love you,
I believe in you
still.

Your suffering –
it is happening to us.
Jesus,
I love you more than life.

God, please take my child to yourself,
and although it is not in vain,
end this torture of us all,

for we are finished.

Jesus Dies

There was a written notice above him, which read: This is the King of the Jews. ... One of the criminals who hung there hurled insults at him: "Aren't you the Messiah? Save yourself and us!" Then he said, "Jesus, remember me when you come into your kingdom. " Jesus answered him, "Truly I tell you, today you will be with me in paradise." It was now about noon, and darkness came over the whole land until three in the afternoon, for the sun stopped shining. And the curtain of the temple was torn in two. Jesus called out with a loud voice, "Father, into your hands I commit my spirit." When he had said this, he breathed his last. (Lk23:38-39,42-46. See also Jn19:26-27; Mt27:45-54; Mk15:33-39).

Not Just Any Man

The most precious gift we can offer anyone is our attention.[15]

Jesus is nailed to the cross. He is offered wine and gall. I remember that he said he would not drink again until he is in the kingdom of the Father. Drink is about sharing, communing. Where is the communion here?

I see Mary at the foot of the cross. She places a damp cloth over Jesus' painful feet. It is a mixture of sting and cool for him. He sees her love and her concern. He says nothing but feels everything. Mary's companion weeps. Her presence moves Jesus but he has no energy for words. He has a heart of compassion for his mother and her friend, and yet he is aggrieved by those who deserted him. He has no thought or energy to blame them. He understands their fear and their rejection.

Even in this darkest hour, when trust has an edge of madness, Jesus puts his trust in God. Jesus is not just any man. Jesus changed peoples' lives. He healed, he forgave, he loved. And here on the cross, he trusts in God.

Need to Understand

Mary, I try to feel how it must have been for you as you looked at your precious son Jesus on that cross. I can only imagine how helpless, angry and distraught you must have felt. But you stayed there. What a gift to him you were. With God's great strength, you were sustained. You were open to God. Always open.

Were you ever able to speak of that experience?

Mary's Pain

> *We are not powerless in the oppressive situations in which we feel caught. We are not bound to the reality we see. We are creators. We can make new.* [16]

It was a hideous thing to watch Jesus suffer unjustly. I felt love and anger together. I never gave in to the evil thrust upon him, even though I finally accepted that I was not able to rescue him. I shed tears in agony. I screamed out: My God please choose another way.

Then something strange happened to me as I looked at Jesus' amazing face. A dignity emerged in my powerlessness. It was the dignity which emerged from knowing that God's love was all that mattered – *Not my will but yours be done.* Jesus retained the power of dignity as he kept his face turned towards God. I came to it gradually; I said yes again.

Later I reflected that all human life begins with a spirit yielding to a greater power. Daily I live in God's presence. Daily I yield to God's benevolent power. I cannot live a moment without God's assurance.

I ask God that you may live and end your life with Jesus' attitude of heart. *Your will be done* – I pray that these words will become a longing for you, and in that longing, you will find the joy of God.

Reflect and Respond

The passion of Jesus is an invitation to respond to injustice. It can make us notice the needy and oppressed. It can make us see where we are all oppressed and needy. I am my brother. I am my sister.

Silent

Mary watched
her word entombed.

In the Rain

words
spill over the gutters

speak of you
hear
the questions
in the rhythm
can you

raise yourself
come
from the tomb
can you

lay yourself on the earth
feel the power in gentle
reassurance

Revelation

*You are the deep innerness of all things, the last word that can be spoken.
To each of us you reveal yourselves differently.*[17]
— Rainer Maria Rilke

Mary at Home

Go home woman.

> No.
> I wait for God's promise.

He laughs.

> Beelzebub!

> God help me.
> Give me hope.
> I need to be raised.
> Jesus.

Go home, woman.

> No.
> I am his mother.
> In this grief at this moment,
> I am most myself.

> I am at home
> waiting.

Risen

Now is your time of grief, but I will see you again and you will rejoice, and no one will take away your joy. (Jn16:22).

After the Sabbath, at dawn on the first day of the week, Mary Magdalene and the other Mary went to look at the tomb. There was a violent earthquake, for an angel of the Lord came down from heaven and, going to the tomb, rolled back the stone and sat on it. His appearance was like lightning, and his clothes were white as snow. The guards were so afraid of him that they shook and became like dead men. The angel said to the women, "Do not be afraid, for I know that you are looking for Jesus, who was crucified. He is not here; he has risen, just as he said. Come and see the place where he lay. Then go quickly and tell his disciples: He has risen from the dead and is going ahead of you into Galilee. There you will see him. Now I have told you." So the women hurried away from the tomb, afraid yet filled with joy, and ran to tell his disciples. (Mt28:1-8; See also 28:9-10; Lk24:1-12; Mk16:1-15).

Faithful Women

> *At night ... when I lie in my bed and rest in you, Oh God, tears of gratitude run down my face, and that is my prayer. ... Things come and go in a deeper rhythm and people must be taught to listen; it's the most important thing we have to learn in this life.*[19]

In the synoptic gospels, we find that the first news of Jesus' resurrection comes to the women who are instructed to go quickly to tell the other disciples. As prayer was her way of life, Mary the mother of Jesus waited for this, God's revelation. In the Spiritual Exercises, Ignatius imagines that at the resurrection, Jesus first appeared to his mother. Let us wonder how this might have happened.

Faithful Mary

Jesus rises from the cold surface of death. He moves through the place where evil overwhelmed him. It has now become quiet. At dawn, it is still. Mary, his mother, is outside the tomb. She has risen from a sleepless night, and put on the shoes Jesus gave her as a gift. She still wears yesterday's faded light-weight dress, over which she has put her mantle of grey wool. She has eaten nothing. Although there is no logic in hurrying, she runs to reach the tomb of her son as soon as possible.

In the dawn haze, she sees Jesus. She is confused. She looks towards the tomb then returns her gaze to Jesus. She is drawn to the marks on his forehead which stand out in the light which seems to emanate from him. Mary is taken into the light as she gazes upon her son. She wants to cover her eyes but she cannot.

Mary knows that Jesus was born for this moment. She also is convicted that her own life has been meaningful. Jesus stands before her – takes her hands and closes them together. She cannot bear to move.

Mary Speaks

You are my son, my love, my life.

Reflect and Respond

[W]hoever lives by believing in me will never die. Do you believe this?" (John 11:26).

Mary's Prayer

Joy,
your breadth and depth and wonder
holds me in consoling certainty.
I leap from my child to my God,
from love's beginning to love eternal.

I long to keep on loving
while love transforms
Love is enough
forever.

She Who Saw

empty
hearts open to beat
with hope
that Jesus lives
as he said.

empty words
we do not know
empty trappings of death
wound up in the corner
where they have laid him
empty tomb
we do not know

who is he,
the other disciple
with quickened heart
ahead of feet?

who is she,
who knew not
who saw
who believed?

An Appearance to the Disciples

On the evening of that first day of the week, when the disciples were together, with the doors locked for fear of the Jewish leaders, Jesus came and stood among them and said, "Peace be with you!" After he said this, he showed them his hands and side. The disciples were overjoyed when they saw the Lord. Again Jesus said, "Peace be with you! As the Father has sent me, I am sending you." And with that he breathed on them and said, "Receive the Holy Spirit. If you forgive anyone's sins, their sins are forgiven; if you do not forgive them, they are not forgiven." (Jn20:19-23; see also Lk24:36-49).

A Room Like This

The disciples had gathered. They were confused and distressed. One paced the floor. Another complained. One sat with her eyes closed. Another stared silently at the wall. One ate voraciously while another picked over his food. Although it was early in the evening, the animals had already come inside. They nestled closely to each other.

Nathaniel had begun to lead the group in prayer when Jesus made his sudden appearance.

Peace and Forgiveness

Jesus knew that nothing but his peace would be sufficient to calm the grief and anxiety which disempowered the disciples in the days following his death.

When Jesus appears to them, he offers his peace. Their response is one of joy. But Jesus looks into their hearts, and again says 'peace be with you'. Peace is part of discipleship. We are shown here in Mark's gospel the relationship between peace, discipleship and the Holy Spirit. The Holy Spirit enables the disciples to forgive. There is no peace without forgiveness. There is no peace without trust in the indwelling Spirit of God.

In Mary's Heart – 15

Merciful God, I am joyful in seeing Jesus, hearing his words, feeling his touch. He speaks of love and forgiveness, and how they are important to well-being. He reminds us that the good news has its foundation on love and forgiveness.

Strange words though: 'for those whose sins you forgive, they are forgiven; for those whose sins you retain, they are retained'. I am certain that if I do not forgive others, sin is retained in myself. Just as we share sin, we share also in God's power to forgive.

Reflect and Respond

What behaviour is difficult for you to forgive? Can you receive forgiveness?

Jesus at God's Right Hand

After the Lord Jesus had spoken to them, he was taken up into heaven and he sat at the right hand of God. Then the disciples went out and preached everywhere, and the Lord worked with them and confirmed his word by the signs that accompanied it. (Mk16:19-20; see also Lk24:50-51; Mt28:18-20).

Faith and Hope

Jesus appeared many times to his disciples in the days following his resurrection. How are we to imagine what he looked like?

The gospel writers want us to know that he was visible, that he was able to eat, that he bore the marks of his suffering. And yet we also read that Jesus appeared to move through substance without conforming to the rules which govern matter.

How Jesus was taken up into heaven is a mystery. Heaven is a mystery. It is a mystery in which we hope to share. Perhaps you already know something of the mystery of heaven and the mystery of being one with Christ in the world. You might also know something of resurrection.

We know that Jesus instructed his disciples, then blessed them before he departed from them. This anointing enabled them to become proclaimers of God's truth.

The disciples testify to Christ's Ascension to God's right hand, but it often feels that Jesus Christ is ascending and descending in our hearts much of the time! We ask to be filled with peace and joy at his abiding presence. We ask to stay focused on him so that we can follow his way, and be more than mere imitators of Christ for the sake of others. We are to be Christ in the world.

Mary Says Goodbye to Jesus

Jesus, I was distraught in the whole experience of watching you suffer. Relief came when you died. Your personal suffering was over. How confused I felt.

When I saw you again, I was caught up in the joy of your presence.

Now that you are leaving Jesus, I am feeling some anxiety. It is not easy to let go. I must look at your life and your promises. If I look at your suffering, too often I am caught up in my own. I don't want to be a half-hearted disciple.

I will look to you Jesus; I will believe that you will be with me always. When I pray this way, I experience God finding a space in my heart. Even my suffering is held in love.

I say yes again.

Reflect and Respond

What is your experience of God in the grief and loss of your life?

Can you say anything about the experience of joy?

Peace I Leave with You

Peace I leave with you; my peace I give you. I do not give to you as the world gives. Do not let your hearts be troubled and do not be afraid. (Jn14:27)

Mary Speaks to Jesus

I need some quiet space, Jesus. There are many things to sort out in my mind about all that has happened. I remember your words, so often said, 'peace be with you'. There is no peace like your peace, but sometimes I need to dig deeply into myself to find it. It is lonely without you. I never expected to bury you, my son.

I have fewer friends now. I used to enjoy sharing with the women when I went to draw water, but now they hurry away when they see me. I know why. It is difficult to be around a widow, even more, a widow whose son has been crucified. Many do not know what to say. Some are ashamed of me. Some are embarrassed that I continue to believe in you. I am not ashamed. I know truth. In fact I abhor the system which tried to silence you, Jesus.

Today I feel my weakness. Somehow it connects me to you. I feel your love. It strengthens me. The difficulty of my life since you have gone has caused me to think about the many decisions I have made which have led to this day. I am who I am because of all the circumstances, choices and decisions of my life. Difficult situations have always challenged me to reflect and to trust more completely in God. In pondering these things, I become aware that God is trusting and believing in me to face the challenges of life. Perhaps it is in these things that I touch a little of what enabled you to walk your life in dignity with steadfast focus.

As I reflect, I notice there are certain things I do and particular friendships I have which make me more sure of myself. I have decided to give energy to these things and to nurture friendships which seem to be good for me.

I thought that my awareness of you Jesus, might diminish as time passes but this is not the case. I see you in the kindness of neighbours who invite me to eat with them or who ask me to help in preparing their family celebrations. In fact I see you in everything. This vision has given me a reason to keep going.

Jesus, you are my child. You always will be. You have taught me how to be a child of God. You have shown me how to be a mother and a friend. You have shown me how to let go of you. Now I dare to seek God's desires for the next phase of my life.

Again my God, I await your angel. 'Do not be afraid . . . The Lord is with you . . . you have found favor with God'.

In Mary's Heart – 16

I know nothing separates me from you God. Within this awareness, I understand what 'being in God' and 'God in us' mean. I don't have words enough to describe this knowing. Peace, belonging, serenity, life; all these are approximations. In this place, I am strong.

I want all people to come to you. I pray that they will know what 'full of grace' means.

God of blessing, bring your beloved children into the fullness of your joy and love.

(See Rom8:31-39)

Reflect and Respond

Imagine God's joy when you respond to the call to prayer.

The Presence of the Holy Spirit

When the day of Pentecost came, they were all together in one place. Suddenly a sound like the blowing of a violent wind came from heaven and filled the whole house where they were sitting. They saw what seemed to be tongues of fire that separated and came to rest on each of them. All of them were filled with the Holy Spirit and began to speak in other tongues as the Spirit enabled them. ... Then Peter stood up with the Eleven, raised his voice and addressed the crowd: "Fellow Jews and all of you who live in Jerusalem, let me explain this to you; listen carefully to what I say. These people are not drunk, as you suppose. It's only nine in the morning! No, this is what was spoken by the prophet Joel: " 'In the last days, God says, I will pour out my Spirit on all people. Your sons and daughters will prophesy, your young men will see visions, your old men will dream dreams. (Acts2:1-4,14-17).

Jesus Christ in Conversation with Us

I will fill your house with my presence. The fire warms. It brings neither fear nor destruction. It is the fire of my love. I have put it in your heart. Let it burn deeply. May your life be one with my life. Stand firm in holiness.

Love and truth are safeguards against the temptations towards evil. Speak from your heart. Stand in your truth. Be aware of my grace. It is sufficient for all situations. Welcome me as you welcome 'the stranger' in your midst, in your home.

Affirm each other's gifts. Look for wisdom in those who have suffered.

And what of Mary, my God? Who might she be to me?

Mary is my loved mother. She can show you how to pray. She will join with you, holding your hands in hers, looking at you and loving you as she loved me. She has enough love for all of you. She longs to unite her prayers with yours towards peace and love. Remember I live on the margins of the world. I live within the world of pain and poverty. Those who hunger are close to my heart.

I wish to transform all hearts from deception and fear to truth and love. I long for you to know of my abiding love and truth.

Abide in me.

Reflect and Respond

Can you describe your personal sense of the presence of Jesus? Can you describe discipleship?

Naming God

Spirit come.
Fill my heart with fire,
the felt-knowledge of truth.
Enable me to be effective
towards the fullness of love.

Christ in recognizing your face,
may I remember to follow you.
May I co-create with you
in this call that I have heard.
May it be carried out in your love,
your strength and grace.

There is nothing I can do without you, God.
Expand my love, joy, peace and patience.

I pray that we may be one.

May all the cosmos
to be united with you
loving creator God.

Glory be to you God of love.

Prayer

Then the apostles returned to Jerusalem from the hill called the Mount of Olives, a Sabbath day's walk from the city. When they arrived, they went upstairs to the room where they were staying. Those present were Peter, John, James and Andrew; Philip and Thomas, Bartholomew and Matthew; James son of Alphaeus and Simon the Zealot, and Judas son of James. They all joined together constantly in prayer, along with the women and Mary the mother of Jesus, and with his brothers. (Acts1:12-14)

Companion Mary Prays

Holy God, I want to be a companion to your children for all time. I know the struggles they are going through.

Because your hand has strengthened me, I am blessed forever in every way which matters. I am your handmaid. I experience your love for me. I am to be esteemed because I am your child. You created me knowing that I would say 'yes' to whatever you asked of me. On that sacred day when I became aware of your Spirit within, I was seeking your word upon my life. I did not understand then what 'the word became flesh' would mean for me.

You called me to motherhood and now to companionship with all. I want to love and be a part of the gathering. I am happy for my life to teach everyone as I taught Jesus. Let me be an abiding companion with Jesus to everyone. One day, may we all share in your goodness which is Love in the fullness of your holy Presence. Until that day, may I pray with everyone seeking your peace on earth.

I adore you my God. My soul magnifies you my God. My spirit leaps with joy at the thought of your love.

Reflect and Respond

What specific vocation or gift has God given you which gives you joy? Think about other gifts you have but have been reluctant to share. What will it take to say 'yes' to that gift?

God

You speak to me.
You are close.
I hear as words from my deepest self.
From here I am to be healed,
created and consoled.

Let me feel living waters
splash upon my skin, my heart.
Drench me in your passion
and the gift of you.
Lord teach me who I am in you.
Hold me strong
and don't let go
even when I do.

Keep my eyes, open, shut,
transfixed to you and your eternal desire.
I am certain
that you will draw me to yourself
because you are Love's Self,
who delights
in the simplest murmuring of praise
which I and he and she and they
cannot help but hum.

With You Jesus

Send me out, Jesus
to be the best I can.
Make clear to me
my poverty and rank
so I may be with you
in the poor,
oppressed
and marginalized,
and they with you in me.

Reflect and Respond

- What is your image of God? How do you experience God towards you or with you?

- What is Mystery?

- What kind of prayer is meaningful for you?

- Can you have a conversation with God about your deepest desires?

- Do you pray for those you love? If so, how?

- Can you relate with the call to be Christ in the world? If so, what does it mean for you?

- What gifts do you have that inspire or motivate you towards love and freedom?

- How is Mary an ordinary woman?

About The Author

Marlene is Australian and married with two adult children and one grandchild.

She has a background in medical imaging, secondary education and post-graduate spiritual direction formation. She is a giver of the Spiritual Exercises. Her PhD awarded in 2014 was entitled *Poetry and Grace: An Autoethnography Exploring Poetry as Prayer in the context of Ignatian Spirituality*. Marlene is a co-founder of Kardia Formation Pty Ltd in Hawthorn, Australia. www.kardia.com.au

Marlene's poetry and essays have been published in various anthologies and journals in Australia and overseas.

Also by The Author

My Brother, My Sister, My Country
Marburg, M., & Sietzema-Dickson, J. (Eds.).
Mont Albert North: Poetica Christi Press. 2005.

Grace Undone : Love (Vol. 1)
Marburg, M., Melbourne: Windsor Scroll. 2014.

Grace Undone : Encounter (Vol. 2)
Marburg, M., Melbourne: Windsor Scroll. 2016.

Grace Undone : Passion (Vols. 3 and 4)
Marburg, M., Melbourne: Windsor Scroll. 2015.

Dreams and Desires : An Anthology of Poetry and Prose
Marburg, M. (Ed.). 40 contributors.
Melbourne. Windsor Scroll. 2016.

References

1. Day, Dorothy. *On Pilgrimage.* Grand Rapids, Michigan: William Eerdmans Publishing, 1999. 1948 by Catholic Worker Books. 30.

2. Fleming, David L. *Draw Me into your Friendship: The Spiritual Exercises, a Literal Translation and a Contemporary Reading.* Saint Louis, Missouri: The Institute of Jesuit Sources. 1996.

3. Hooper, Rose rc. "Ordinary Holiness." In *Caught up in God*, edited by Sisters of the Cenacle, 7 April 2005. http://www.vocationquest.org/cenacle/2005/04/07/ordinary-holiness/ Accessed 1 January 2017.

4. Oliver, Mary. Upstream. New York: Penguin Press, 2016. 8.

5. Oliver, Mary. "When Death Comes." In *New and Selected Poems: Volume One* (1991-1992). Boston, Massachusetts: Beacon Press Books, 1992. 10.

6. Chesterton, Gilbert K. BrainyQuote.com, Xplore Inc, 2017. https://www.brainyquote.com/quotes/quotes/g/gilbertkc107505.html, accessed January 1. 2017.

7. Oliver, Mary. Upstream. New York: Penguin Press, 2016. 5.

8. Oliver, Mary. "When I Am among Trees." In Thirst. Boston Massachusetts: Beacon Press, 2006. 4.

9. Hanh, Thich Nhat. Fear: *Essential Wisdom for Getting through the Storm.* London: Rider, 2012. 164.

10. David Whyte. AZQuotes.com, Wind and Fly LTD, 2017. http://www.azquotes.com/quote/810566, accessed 1 January 2017.

11. Chesterton, G.K. "The Maniac." In *Orthodoxy: The Fundamentalist Argument*. United States of America: MSAC Philosophy Group, 2008. 9.

12. "Rumi: Join the Great Song." edited by Michael Meade, 3:30. https://www.youtube.com/watch?v=b0PvpnE8dN8&feature=youtu.be: Mosaic Voices.

13. Coelho, Paul. *The Alchemist: A Graphic Novel*. Hardback ed. New York: HarperOne, 2010.

14. Chesterton, G. K. *The Man Who Was Orthodox: A Selection from the Uncollected Writings of G. K. Chesterton* Hardcover ed. London: Dennis Dobson, 1963 (originally from a daily newspaper in 1905).

15. Hanh, Thich Nhat, and Adam Guan (artwork). "January Quote." In *Thich Nhat Hanh: 2016 Calendar*: Brush Dance, 2015.

16. O'Connor, Elizabeth. *Cry Pain, Cry Hope: Thresholds to Purpose*. Nashville: W. Publishing Group, 1987.

17. Rilke, Rainer Maria. Du bist die Zukunft, grosses Morgenrot (You are the Future, the great Sunrise red – for one translation title, see: https://thefloatinglibrary.com/2010/01/02/you-are-the-future-the-great-sunrise-red/) *Book of Hours*. Text of poem translated by Anita Barrows and Joanna Macy. New York: Riverhead Books, 1996. 119.

18. Hillesum, Etty, and Arnold J. Pomerans (Translator). "60. To Henny Tideman. Westerbork Wednesday 18 August 1943." In *The Letters and Diaries of Etty Hillesum*, 1941-1943, edited by Klaas A. D. Smelik, 640: Wm. B. Eerdsman Publishing, 2002.

www.ingramcontent.com/pod-product-compliance
Lightning Source LLC
Chambersburg PA
CBHW060516300426
44112CB00017B/2700